How to Expand Your Small Business: The Definitive Guide to Growing Your Small Business Successfully

By

Maurice Chavez

Copyright © 2019

All rights reserved. No portion of the book may be reproduced or utilized in any form or by any means, electronic or mechanical, including photocopying, recording, or by any other information storage and retrieval system, without express written permission from the author.

Table of Contents

Introduction	4
Marketing off the Beaten Track	7
Raising Money in the Clouds	15
Optimizing the Day-to-Day	22
You, Your Business, and the Law	39
Conclusion	49
APPENDIX	50
TOP CROWDFUNDING WEBSITES	52
BIBLIOGRAPHY	53

Introduction

Congratulations!

You have taken your business beyond the first step. You have created a product or service that the marketplace wants. You have consequently been rewarded with a decent sales volume, which is allowing you to pursue your dream full-time. You may even be at the point where it will be important to hire staff to help you. This is all part of becoming a successful entrepreneur.

While you do have the right to give yourself a pat on the back, you must be ready for the next step on the path to full success in the marketplace. This next move is going to be a very important one. Unless you wish to have a boutique shop, or deliberately desire to stay small, you will want to expand upon your foundation. This is going to mean reaching out to a larger audience, competing with others for market share, and spreading the word about what it is that you have to offer. Efficiency is going to become increasingly important in the internal operations and administration of your company. You are going to have to find ways to finance your expansion beyond the profit margins that are sales-generated. It should come as no surprise to you that the mistakes you once tolerated are no longer acceptable. This is all part of going to the next level as a company and a business owner. If you want to continue down the road to success, you have to do what is necessary.

This book is intended to be a helpful resource for you. The topics we cover are important for an entrepreneur who is looking to take his or her business to the next level. What we will be discussing are those key activities and ideas that we consider to be the most cost-effective. It goes without saying that these are also considered highly efficient. The modern global economy has created amazing opportunities for an entrepreneur. Many of the advances in business, technology, and practices of the last 10 years have leveled the playing field; the "little guy" can now successfully compete with larger companies. The challenges entrepreneurs faced years ago have been eradicated, thanks to the Internet and mobile applications. Certain business practices that were laughed at just a few years ago are taken quite seriously now.

Right now, you may happen to be sailing along on a favorable current with the wind filling your sails. Amazing ride so far, isn't it? Therefore, there is something you really should resist as you go through this eBook. When you read the various ideas and suggestions, you may say to yourself, "Duh, why didn't I think of that earlier?!" The reason you didn't was quite simple: you were thinking of more important things at the time. The initial steps of setting up a business require attention to some very fundamental activities, such as setting up a line of credit or filing necessary government papers. You now have the opportunity to start thinking about other things that will work together to grow your business.

The parable of the mustard seed can apply to a certain degree with new start-ups. It is very possible that a business will suddenly shoot up, only to wither before long. However, those companies that are built on strong foundations and solid business practices are going to be extremely successful as time goes by. This book is intended to help you solidify the foundations you've already created and to let you move forward with confidence. Always remember that you are now at the point where you are actually living your dream. This book will attempt to equip you with tools that can help you make that dream into a bigger, more exciting reality.

Marketing off the Beaten Track

You must accept the fact that you will be spending a considerable amount of time involved in marketing activities. You are still establishing your brand identity in the public eye, and that is going to take some effort. Entrepreneurs often feel somewhat nervous about this. They start having nightmarish visions of advertising budgets that are astronomical in cost and cut into profits. These expenses are prices that need to be paid in order to keep your business growing. Admittedly, this is an old-school concern, but, lucky for you, this is not your father's marketplace.

At the second level, you do not have to spend a lot of energy on traditional marketing such as print media and television commercials. Yes, there is no question that these are important parts of any marketing ploy, but timing is important, too. Until your sales volume shows a healthy increase along with a good profit margin, you should consider some other options. These, by the way, cost less than the ordinary television commercial or print ad.

1. The Old Standbys Work!

A. T-Shirts, Coffee Mugs, and Other Neat Stuff

Brand promotion strategies can be amazingly simple. While some start-up companies may want to invest money in sharp-looking television advertisements, we must think about why they are doing it. It may not be for brand promotion alone, but ego enhancement as well. A business owner may feel a great deal of satisfaction in seeing a television advertisement promoting his or her brand and company. The flipside is that those advertisements only last for a certain amount of time. Therefore, there is no guarantee of long-term memories about your company.

The old standbys are actually some of the most effective brand promotion tactics you can use at this point in your corporate history. T-shirts and coffee mugs may sound a bit amateurish to some people, but those folks don't understand being cost-effective. T-shirts don't cost much. Neither do coffee mugs. You can buy these in bulk and place a catchy-looking logo on the product. Here is where the benefit is going to be realized.

It's all in brand promotion. These promotional products parade your business in front of the buying public as often as possible. Anybody who wears your T-shirt is a walking billboard for your product and company. What really helps is that people will wear T-shirts for months or even years after they first receive one. This means that pedestrian traffic in particular is going to keep your product in clear sight for a rather long time. If you are selling a product or service that is business-oriented, a coffee mug in a cubicle lets the right people know that you exist. It is important to make sure that contact information, particularly your website address, is part of that brand logo.

B. Looking Good in the Neighborhood

Society has changed over the last few years and now holds certain expectations that corporate entities need to address. Social responsibility and community awareness, as well as an understanding that businesses must give something back to the neighborhood, have become extremely important. In fact, people will base their spending habits in part on whether or not they perceive that a business is truly involved in social welfare. This is where those old standbys are really going to help.

Charities sponsor all kinds of events: races, walkathons, and other events that generate both awareness and donations. You can be a part of this, to the benefit of your company. If you are approached by a charity to be a sponsor, be sure to ask if your logo will be put on any of the T-shirts or paraphernalia that are part of the event. This allows you to not only broadcast your brand, but also to be identified with a very worthwhile cause. That is going to help develop the kind of community-sensitive awareness that your company needs. You should also ask about the charity event website, and whether or not your logo will be on the first page. That is another way to announce your brand in a very positive light.

2. Rocking the Internet

Every successful entrepreneur appreciates the importance of Internet marketing. The ability to potentially reach millions of customers and clients is there, and has been written about extensively. You are no doubt already using the Internet and perhaps you are even an account holder of various social media platforms. The challenge now is to be able to use those platforms as effectively as possible.

The shotgun approach, having numerous social media accounts, is not necessarily the most effective social media marketing strategy. As you look at costs, you have to remember that time can be just as important as money. You must be able to spend your precious minutes effectively.

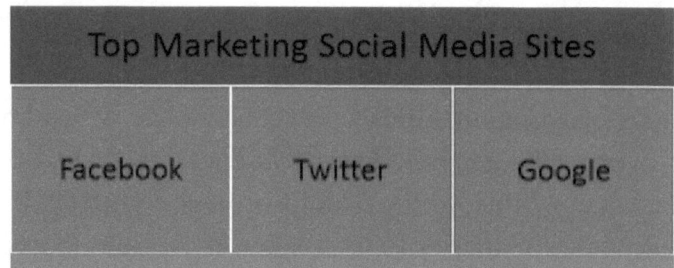

This means that more time and attention should be spent on those platforms that are best suited to promote your brand.

A. Appreciate the Demographics

> Social media has been around long enough to measure demographics. We know by now that certain platforms will appeal to given groups. You need to pay attention to those whose audiences most nearly resemble your primary base of

customers. Here are some of the more popular social media platforms and their primary demographics:

- Pinterest is growing rapidly on mobile applications and accounts for 48.2% of all social media sharing on iPads. Products of interest are primarily pictures of food and drink related content.

- For anyone under the age of 35, Instagram is the picture base of choice (90% of all account holders are under 35 years old). This platform is a must for anyone marketing entertainment and media brands focusing on the 18 – 34 age range.

- Don't bother posting on Twitter after 3 PM on a Friday; it is a waste of time. The best time to tweet is Monday through Thursday between 1 PM and 3 PM. This is additionally a platform that is used most often in urban areas.

- Facebook is not necessarily a good place to advertise luxury goods. The population of Facebook is still fairly young. On the other hand, fast-moving consumer goods do well there, and Facebook users account for half of all promotional-related clicks on the Internet.

- LinkedIn has a high-income, highly educated user base. If you want to get connected to this crowd, consider Tuesday through Thursday at the start and end of the workday.

- Tumblr is definitely for kids, and 61% of teenagers (13-18 years old) make use of it for several hours a week (Smith, 2014).

You can generate leads using social media platforms. It is even possible to have ads placed that can generate the kind of business you are hoping to receive. Once again, it is important to focus attention on those platforms that can provide the best results. Statistics provide some excellent guides:

- 70% of marketers use Facebook to get new customers.
- Facebook, Twitter, and Google are the top 3 social media sites marketers use.
- 34% of marketers use Twitter to successfully generate leads.
- 70% of brands have a presence on Google+.

The data can also give you an idea of what sites are just not worth your time. Flickr and Stumbleupon are among the social media sites that marketers generally ignore (Bullas, 2014).

B. Consider the Content

You must be very careful about using social media platforms for marketing alone. Other people don't appreciate that, and it can lose you followers on Twitter. Over and over again, the mantra "Content is King" can be heard. Social media experts write blog after blog about the need for great content. It is suggested that you become an expert source in order to attract a following of dedicated customers. The catch always seems to be where to find all of this great information with which to impress. Believe it or not, this is easier done than said.

Media platforms, such as Reuters, have information feeds that you can connect to your Twitter account or other platforms. This provides a constant stream of news that people can access. Another great place to get that information-rich content is

Feedly.com. The beauty of this particular website is that it deals with all kinds of information. You can easily access entertainment, fashion, world news, and other content sources. Feedly will allow you to directly link a particular story to your Twitter, Facebook, Google+, LinkedIn, and several other social media accounts. It means that you can have fresh content nearly 24/7, if that is what you would like.

Another source of content are the communities on Google+. This particular platform, by the way, is a great place to interact with like-minded people and share information.

C. Google Marketing

Google has paved the way in online marketing and continues to go out of its way to help people market their products. Google AdWords is something worth knowing about, whether you are ready to use it yet or not. It is a pay-per-click service where you can create ads for your business, and these ads are displayed in Google search results. There are many benefits that this Google service offers, one of which is the ability to have a better control over your advertising costs. The reason for this is that you are able to set a maximum cost per day for a given campaign. If necessary, you can also increase your budget.

Google AdWords will help you in the never-ending battle with your competition. By aligning yourself with a Google product, you will have exposure on the biggest search engine in the global economy. This means you will get quite a few clicks on your ads. Google is definitely a tool to be used when you are ready to move into placing Internet advertisements (Rampton, 2014).

There are some other things you should be aware of when it comes to marketing, and these will be discussed later on in the book. They deal a bit more with how to best administer your marketing, especially when it comes to working on social media platforms.

Raising Money in the Clouds

Commonly referred to as the Great Recession, the financial crisis of 2008 created severe difficulties for small businesses that still have not been completely resolved. In the time period of 2008 to 2011, lending to small businesses dropped 18 percent. Banks are now incredibly risk-adverse and hesitate to take any chances. The lending standards of traditional financial institutions have consequently been tightened, and a small business loan has become extremely difficult to obtain (National Funding, 2013).

This creates a harsh situation for many entrepreneurs. Their first round of funding may have been personal savings, loans or gifts from family, or even a small business loan that cannot be renewed. An environment that is strapped for cash makes it extremely difficult to expand, or even meet, current expenses. You may have to consider other sources for needed funds, and this is where you'll need to get creative. The good thing is that the present environment can also reward an individual for thinking outside the box. If the bank down the street cannot provide you with a loan you need, perhaps it may be time to go looking in the clouds for that seed money.

A. Checking out the Crowd

Entrepreneurs in the United States received a significant amount of assistance when the Jumpstart Our Business Startups Act (JOBS Act) was signed into law. This showed recognition by the federal government that small businesses, particularly start-ups, play a major role in job creation in the new economy. The act allows these new business establishments to raise money through crowd-funding efforts.

There are already some websites that have been established to assist in crowd-funding. Kickstarter and Indigogo.com come to mind immediately. The premise is very simple. An entrepreneur sets up a campaign on a crowd-funding site. The intended amount of money to be raised is stated, and an explanation of the campaign is given. The entrepreneur provides incentives, in the form of rewards, for given levels of donation. This is something very important to keep in mind. As of this writing, donors primarily receive perks (Sareen, 2013).

Entrepreneurs who sell shares in their companies via crowd-funding can raise no more than $1 million in a 12-month cycle, or else they must deal with the Securities Exchange Commission and the agency's securities registration requirements (Fallon, 2014).

The donations are ordinarily in small amounts, $100 or less. The money is raised by a volume of donors, which can be incredibly large. The smart-watch company Pebble Watches was able to raise the amount of $10 million from approximately 69,000 donors. That is an incredible amount, but it is also out of the ordinary. Most entrepreneurs can expect to raise far smaller sums of money (Arora, 2012).

Entrepreneurs who are considering the use of crowd-funding must understand that there is some administrative work and planning involved. It makes absolutely no sense to post a crowd-funding campaign without having any idea of what to do. The monetary goal has to be realistic and attainable. Moreover, the requirements of a given crowd-funding platform have to be examined. There is the possibility of "loser gives up all," should the campaign goal not be reached. Having to refund donors is embarrassing, to say the very least. There is also a need to generate interest. If an entrepreneur already has a following, it can be little bit easier to raise the needed money (Fallon, Crowdfunding Challenges Most Startups Don't Expect, 2014). (HINT: This is where developing your Twitter following is really going to help. If you have a large number of followers, you can direct them to the crowd-funding website.)

Crowd-funding does hold some opportunities for entrepreneurs if they are ready. The government appreciates the lack of knowledge an average entrepreneur may have regarding crowd-funding, and the Small Business Administration offers an [online training course](#) to help. A little research and information gathering at a time will do a lot to assure that any venture into crowd-funding is successful.

B. Peer to Peer Lending

This is another consequence of the 2008 financial disaster. Peer to peer lending is done on websites such as Lending Club.com and Prosper.com. These sites look at the various factors of a prospective borrower, including credit history, and assign a risk score to help develop an interest rate for the proposed loan. Investors search the sites for a loan in which to invest, and then fund it. Besides making use of the Internet, the peer to peer lending deals with unsecured loans, something the banks are no longer interested in considering. These are also fixed-rate loans that will not change. Investors benefit by getting interest rates that are higher than treasury notes or other forms of commercial paper (Blackman, 2014).

P2P Pros	P2P Cons
☐ No bank application	☐ Still a need for financial information
☐ Investor assumes risk	☐ Risk is assigned. Interest could be high.
☐ Money is received quickly	☐ Certain states restrict the amount of the loan

Peer to peer lending places most of the risk on the shoulders of the investor, and interest rates compare favorably with those offered by credit card companies. However, it has to be remembered that there is some spade work to be done. An entrepreneur has to be able to fully outline the reason for the loan and provide financial information to help a potential investor decide. Certain states have guidelines regarding peer to peer lending, and some may have restrictions on the size of the loan. It is a smart idea to check on this before venturing into the peer to peer lending arena.

C. Merchant Cash Advance

The need to obtain financial resources may lead an entrepreneur to consider a merchant cash advance. To a certain degree, this is betting on the future. Essentially, a provider will give an entrepreneur a lump sum payment and receive a share of future credit card sales in return. This arrangement is very attractive to retail stores and restaurants that have considerable credit card sales volume on a daily basis. A percentage of daily sales is given to the provider until the advance, plus a premium, is paid off. This usually happens within one calendar year (Tozzi, 2009). These advances are very easy to qualify for, and, once approved, the applicant will get the advance within a matter of a few days.

A merchant cash advance is an alternative that is thought of in the face of tight loan requirements and time constraints. Many entrepreneurs do not have the kind of collateral needed to get the sizable bank loans necessary for expansion, and they cannot wait weeks for approval. These establishments do have brisk credit card sales and rely on those figures to continue to be steady. The repayment is not a monthly, but rather a daily, occurrence; there is no major end-of-the-month payment (Goodman, 2012).

The pros and cons of a merchant cash advance demonstrate the importance of having a firm handle on the money. An entrepreneur may have operated out of pocket in the early days, but that becomes risky as the business progresses to the next step. You should require a firm idea of cash flow, perhaps on a daily basis, and debt management should be a priority item. Some ideas on how to best monitor your business dollars will be discussed later on in this eBook.

The downside of all this is that a healthy sales volume is required. Providers will point out that, if there are no credit card sales in a given day, there is no payment. That is true, but the debt still remains on the books. That debt burden is not as easy as it may seem. Providers will charge a fee that can be over 50% of the advance; that is in addition to the original sum. An entrepreneur must also consider contingencies that are part of the merchant cash advance. Providers want their money back and will place certain conditions on the agreement that need to be followed. Depending on the provider, these can take some control of the business away from its management for the duration. Failure to adhere to the contingencies can result in breach of contract, which can lead to lawsuits (Rose, 2013).

Incidentally, none of the information in this chapter should be considered as financial advice or recommendations for various courses of action. What is being provided for the reader is information that may or may not be used for raising money. It is up to the reader to decide what course of action to take; we do not suggest any one route over another. It is recommended that the reader seek the opinion of a financial professional or public agency, such as the Small Business Administration, for further guidance.

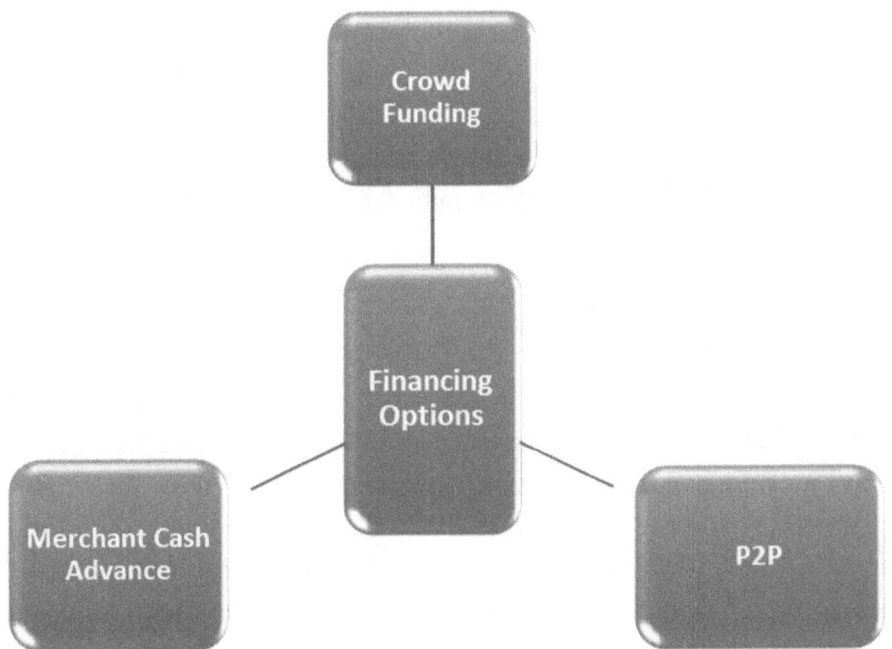

Optimizing the Day-to-Day

Your company has been in the marketplace for some time, and you are used to dealing with the competition. Going to the next level, you will find that competing with rivals gets more and more difficult. Market share is something that is often fought over and must be defended vigorously. You are going to discover that the best way of doing this will be utilizing tight administration and top-notch organization.

Marketing can sometimes be a lot of fun, if the chase is exciting. However, you have to follow up on any order placed or request for service. That is on top of all of the day-to-day activity. If you run your business like a casual hobby or in a disheveled way, you will very soon fail. You need to take advantage of ways to keep the office running smoothly with time efficiency that will enhance productivity. Every hour of every day should be optimized.

A. Mobile Applications to the Rescue!

> Productivity is going to be a primary concern of yours as you move to the next step in your commercial success story. Lucky for you, that productivity happens to be a major theme for mobile applications. These apps help organize not only your personal day, but also the working day of any subordinates you may have. The right mobile applications will not only help you stay on top of things, but also permit you to easily make

changes in direction and correct problems that may come out of nowhere.

Do you notice that I am referring to mobile applications and not to websites? The reason is very simple. Mobile applications have connections to their respective websites. The difference is that people often access websites by means of their PC's or laptops, which are often stationary devices in an office. There is nothing wrong with this, except that when you are on the move, going to a meeting or visiting a client, you may have to get information from an employee or find out the status is of an ongoing project. That is a very simple thing to do when you have a good mobile application on your iPhone or iPad. You can actually be checking on the status of projects at the office while you are waiting in a lobby. The beauty of mobile applications is that they sharply reduce the amount of non-productive time. Here are some of the best apps you should consider to maximize efficiency:

- Deal with the email.
  Those little notes in your email basket can get awfully cumbersome and could certainly use some organization. That is where a Chrome extension called The Email Game can really help. It allows you to put Timers on your inbox and permits you to decide whether a message gets immediate attention or should be saved for later. Mailtracker will send a notification of when and where the other party reads your message. Additionally, shipments of packages can be a very real source of concern. With Google Wallet, you don't have to worry about checking on a delivery status at FedEx because updates are sent to you through the app, including any changes that may occur along the way.

- Keep a handle on expenses.
  This can be critical when it comes to business travel. Expensify will help you track your car mileage and get travel updates. It can also log billable hours. Smartscan will enable you to take pictures of receipts, if you need them, and upload them to an expense report (New Zealand Herald, 2014).

- Organize the team.
  You may be out of the office, or your employees may be running errands. As a matter of fact, your employees may be at a distance because you decided to outsource certain parts of a given project. Keeping them together and on task may seem to be a challenge, but certain mobile applications make things a lot easier. Basecamp allows you to post new assignments, note others' progress, and make everybody aware of the status of the project (Basecamp does require an Internet connection to be used). Evernote can perform comparable organization chores with its notebooks, permitting staff to know the status of projects and also to give updates (Garling, 2014).

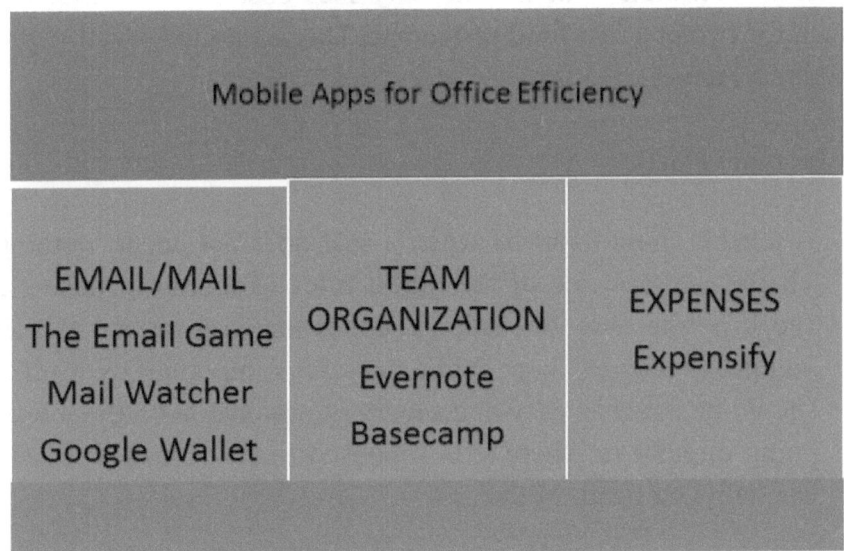

Here is something else to consider while reviewing the usefulness of mobile applications. These applications allow access through smart phones, iPads, templates, laptops, and standard PC's. No matter what you or your employees or colleagues use, you can share information by mobile applications. This takes things one step beyond the ordinary laptop or PC usage. It doesn't matter which medium a person decides to use; project access is there. These mobile applications have demonstrably leveled the playing field. As you step up to the next level, you can do so knowing that you can compete with larger companies.

There are more mobile applications that you might want to consider beyond what has been mentioned. If any of these mobile applications have piqued your interest, you should know that getting them isn't that difficult. If you check the Apps Store of your Android, iOS device, or iPhone, they might just be there waiting for you. Incidentally, you will be pleasantly surprised to know that most of them are free of charge. It is true that there may be a price for going to a higher product level (e.g., moving from

Basic to Premium), but the monthly fees cost about as much as lunch for two at a fast food restaurant. This is certainly well within anyone's budget.

B. Promote Plastic

A terrible thing happens when a sale does not occur: nothing. That is perhaps one of the oldest rules of thumb in business, and it is true. Any one sale generates the cash needed to help you get to the next step. While the sale is important by itself, it should be made as easy and secure as possible, with the money going directly to where it is supposed to be deposited. Plastic can help you do all of that.

- Promote the use of debit and credit cards.
  You will not make it to the next level if you do not encourage the use of credit and debit cards. That is both a warning and a fact. You may have been able to survive the early days with cash and checks only, but you will see less than wonderful sales figures if your customers are not able to use their plastic.

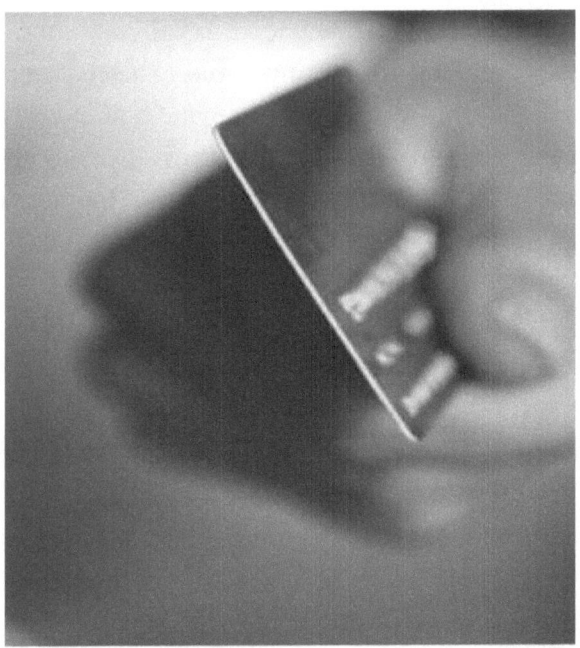

There is a simple logic behind this. People do not like to carry cash, particularly large amounts. You will have a very difficult time selling major appliances or computers on a cash-only basis. Here's something else to think about when it comes to credit and debit cards: people have a habit of spending more than they planned if they are able to use their plastic. If you are able to accept the major credit cards (MasterCard, Visa, Discover Card, etc.), you will undoubtedly reap the benefit of a greater sales volume.

- Do not overlook gift and loyalty cards.
  The time between holidays can be a holy hell for retail shops, and weekdays mean slow business for a lot of restaurants. Gift and loyalty cards can drum up business during these slow periods. Gift cards are loaded with a set amount of money and encourage folks to shop. You can give these out by mail or at the point of sale in your establishment. Loyalty cards are your way of saying thanks

to someone who has been a loyal customer. These cards are also amazing marketing tools. This is something a person will put in a wallet or purse and see every time they check for cash. Gift and loyalty cards can up the sales volume beyond the figure on the plastic. In fact, consumers will spend upwards of 50% more when purchases include using a gift card (Gaul, 2013).

C. Maximize the Point of Sale

It was not so long ago that the point of sale (POS) was a cash register located near the door of a business establishment. The problem with the old-fashioned cash register was not only the fact that employee pilfering was possible. It was also risky to have all of the cash in the register in case of potential robbery, and processing credit cards was not always easy. There was also some lag time between money received by a customer and the deposit into the company bank accounts. The technology behind POS has dramatically improved in the last few years. The equipment is more than just machinery to process a transaction. Point of sale systems perform a variety of tasks that can help you maximize the sale itself and also make financial administration more time- and cost-effective. A POS system is not simply a cash register, but integral software that is intended to make life a whole lot easier for you. Here is why:

- It reduces shrinkage.
  Most employees are honest, but there are a few who have sticky fingers. That is not just at the register, but in the back room, as well. Retail stores are always concerned about shrinkage, the loss of stock due to theft. The only time when this is really noticed is when inventory is taken or when there is a sudden shortage. A good POS system will record sales immediately. It can permit you to track how much is being sold of what items. This will help with managing inventory levels and quickly identify situations where that which is registered on the books does not match what is actually on the storage shelves.

- It enhances customer service opportunities.
  A POS system ordinarily registers sales with the swipe of a barcode. The figures are accurate, and the customer knows immediately how the sums are adding up. The chance of human error on the part of a sales clerk disappears completely. The POS terminal tells the total cost and can determine the change you give back to the customer. While the system is calculating the total sales, the sales associate has the opportunity to demonstrate some customer service skills. This could be pleasant banter with the customer, or perhaps providing information about an upcoming sale. It is all about making the transaction a delight. One thing the customer is certainly going to enjoy is that, with a POS system, waiting for a sale to be completed takes a lot less time than doing it the old-fashioned way (Wuorio, 2014).

- It facilitates reports and analysis.
  The hardest part about being a small business owner is all the long hours spent trying to make sense out of the daily sales figures. A POS system will permit daily sales reports

to be compiled and allow you to spot sales trends, track cashier performance, and even export the reports to an Excel spreadsheet, if necessary. Inventory can be better tracked, and the same is true regarding purchase orders. Some of the POS systems can also maintain customer profiles to allow you to send promotions to a customer based on that person's previous purchasing history (Retail Information Systems, 2014). The sophistication of these reports simply cannot be denied. They tell you more about the sales and purchase patterns of your business than you ever knew before.

- POS equipment will allow you new avenues for sales.
A point of sale terminal is not always the cash register or the card swipe machine at the front desk. There are a number of point of sale models that can expand your sales horizons incredibly. First and foremost is a POS tablet. It can process any transactions that are intended for residential service. You or your employee can actually complete the transaction at the service truck or at the customer's front door. The sales/service is automatically added to the financial records, and you need not call into the office with any information (the POS equipment can also verify credit card numbers, thus saving time and making the transaction even more convenient).

- Handheld POS terminals increase mobility.
These little transactions gadgets are a must for anybody who has a restaurant. Handheld POS terminals permit customer orders to be moved much more quickly. They also allow for better information if the customer has a question about the menu. When it comes time for the transaction, a waiter can very easily perform that right at the table. There is no need to go to a centralized cash

register at all. As restaurant staff start using these handheld gadgets, increased efficiency and performance is noticeable. There are no long lines at the cash register, and transaction activity flows without any problem. The handheld models are also great when your business takes you to trade shows or outdoor markets. You are not tied down to your kiosk, but can move about the crowd. Any sale can be done right on the spot. Shoppers during the holiday season hate having to stand in line. The handheld terminals permit your employees to go up and down the crowded lines, making the point of sale wherever the customer happens to be standing. Needless to say, this keeps the line moving.

One final benefit to these POS terminals is that they are available for smart phones. It is possible for you to get one that can act as a credit card swipe attached to your iPhone or Android. Ring It Up Point of Sale is an example of a credit card terminal you can have attached to your iPhone.

There are a number of companies that offer point of sale equipment to customers. First Data is one such provider, and another is Balboa Capital. A very popular supplier of point of sale systems is QuickBooks. Some of these providers will showcase their equipment to businesses in general, while others will concentrate on niches such as restaurants. Here is a very important tip to keep in mind when it comes to point of sale equipment: do not buy it, lease it!

The POS technology is in an almost constant state of upgrade as manufacturers compete for business. It means that purchased POS equipment can become old-fashioned within months of being bought. It then becomes just another piece of office inventory you need to worry about. When you lease equipment, however, you have its use for one or two years. Just as it is about to become obsolete, the lease is up, and you can negotiate for new, and even better, point of sale technology. A machine is going to break down if it gets a lot of use. Depending on the terms of the lease, the leasing company may provide repair services, or even allow you the use of another machine while the one you have leased is being repaired. It is basically a question of efficiency. Leasing equipment that is continually being improved is simply a very cost-effective approach.

The equipment will allow you some advantages, which you are going to need. The accurate reports allow you to keep a firm hand on the pulse of your business, and the inventory tracking will keep your purchasing activity within budget. Above all, time is the greatest gift point of sale technology is going to give you. Less time will be spent trying to collect data, and less time will be spent doing precise transactions. If you are in retail or the restaurant business, this is the kind of equipment that will get you to the next step without question.

D. Managing the Message

> We discussed earlier the importance of social media marketing. This must be part of the next step in your company's development. The opportunity to expand sales is simply too great to ignore. Moreover, your competition is going to make use of the social media platforms, and you cannot afford to fall behind. The challenge you could be facing is time. Managing your messages over a multitude of websites can be incredibly time-consuming. You also cannot use the same message wording in any two places. LinkedIn is a bit more formal than Twitter, and the demographics of a social media platform must be respected. One central location for message management

would certainly help, and there happens to be one. Its name is HootSuite.

HootSuite is technically a social media management system. In reality, this is a godsend for any small business or entrepreneur. It is a dashboard that permits better management of all social media channels. Any updates or messages to the various platforms, such as Twitter, Facebook, Google+, and LinkedIn, among others, can be done from one location. You will not have to spend precious time going from one site to another; HootSuite can handle it all. You can also delegate various activities and team members, and HootSuite allows messaging back and forth within the team. HootSuite can also provide analytics to help you better understand the activity of the various social networks of which you are a member. What is really great about HootSuite is that it is scalable. It has services ready for you when it is time to make the next step. These will cost a monthly charge, but the time savings you get from using HootSuite makes it worthwhile (Gray, 2014).

E. Reputation Management

Social media was initially developed as a means by which people could share ideas and opinions. It was also a way to share gossip and comments about the quality of service rendered, or products purchased. Public comments about businesses have grown significantly in the last few years. Consumers, by and large, will trust the opinion of other consumers before they believe the advertising of a company. This can put your brand in a rather interesting predicament. The impression consumers have formed and shared with others can have a very powerful effect on your sales volume. Your reputation can be at the mercy of various consumer boards and how you respond to comments. Reputation management is something that is now a very important administrative duty. You cannot ignore it.

By all means, register your company on Yelp. This is the premier review board on the Internet. In the third quarter of 2013, Yelp had over 47.3 million cumulative reviews. What can make Yelp a gold mine for any small business is that a large number of Yelp users are in the mood to make a purchase. Statistics indicate that 35% of Yelp users will make a visit to a searched business within 24 hours of finding it on the review board, with the possibility of making a purchase within a week. In addition to that, the data also indicates that most Yelp reviews are favorable. This is a website you are going to need to broadcast the reputation of your business (LocalVox, 2014).

Once you are established on Yelp, you need to monitor your business's activity. If you see a favorable review, be certain to respond with appreciation. If you see a review that is less than favorable, take this as an opportunity to display superior customer service. Post a response to a problem that shows your recognition of it, and offer a solution. Other visitors to your Yelp page will appreciate your customer sensitivity. Your reputation on Yelp can be further enhanced if you ask loyal patrons and customers to submit a review. It will usually be a good one, as long as you are asking people whom you know had a good experience.

The darker side of a reputation on social media involves your vulnerability in cyberspace. Gossip and comments can be vicious and also untrue. It is possible that unethical competitors will post negative comments about your company. Given that potential customers will read those reviews, you cannot ignore them. They have to be responded to in a highly professional way. This may mean taking advantage of the services of a reputation management company. These professionals have the mission of protecting their clients from negative comments and opinions. They have various ways of doing this.

Some of the defenses are fairly simple. Reputation management professionals will see to it that a well-written biography will dominate your profiles. This can mean that the top links of any Google search for you or your company are highly positive. You will be alerted whenever something ugly about you is posted on the Internet. Reputation managers will also investigate your existing social media accounts, such as Facebook, and warn you of what may be compromising pictures or comments (O'Hara, 2013). They may recommend that you buy a domain name and pay close attention to any profiles you have on various sites. Other tactics may include reporting offensive comments to the website administrator and asking that the negative messages be removed. Cease and desist letters are also means of removing repetition-damaging material.

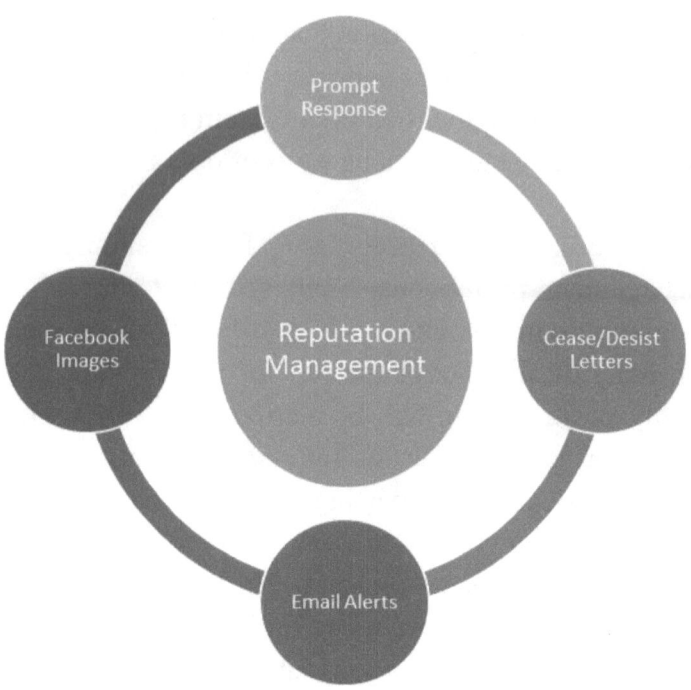

Of course, you can also do a fair amount to protect your reputation. Be careful about using Facebook, and make sure the images you place on your Facebook page are not damaging to you. You can also consider blogging as a means of heightening a positive image. Responding quickly and positively to any instance of vicious comments is going to help considerably. If someone is slamming your product or service on a consumer board, take the opportunity to correct the bad impressions as soon as you can (Conner, 2014).

F. Office Space Made Easy

Your business may have outgrown your home office, and you need to be able to have a place to meet with clients and staff. That could be a problem if you are tight on cash. Even though office space might be available for rent, the cost per square foot may be a real budget-buster. The cost is magnified if the space rented is more than what you need. Don't worry, though; there is a way to get the space you need at a reasonable price.

There are companies that lease space with the small business entrepreneur in mind. Regus is one of them. With 2,000 locations in 750 cities, Regus will provide the office space any small enterprise might need. This could be a private office, short-term space for any task or project, or even temporary space if you need an office for only a few days every month. Conference room space, a phone-answering service, and mail handling can also be part of the package. What the arrangement means is less overhead worries for you. You have exactly the space you need, and there are no wasted desks. In addition, there is no need to be concerned about property-casualty insurance, janitorial service, or security; the leaser takes care of all of that for you, and you don't have those nagging additional costs. More time and effort can be spent on your core business and responding to the needs of customers and clients. All of this is done in an office space sufficient for your needs and flexible enough to best accommodate your time.

G. Outsourcing

Even a small business may be considering doing some outsourcing. This can be an effective means of getting time-sensitive projects done, especially those involving software and mobile application development. There has been a lot of media outcry regarding outsourcing. Without going into the emotions of politics, it needs to be remembered that your next step up is going to rely on being able to efficiently and effectively deliver the goods. Putting the cost of labor aside, outsourcing permits you to work on a project 24/7. For example, as you leave the office in New York City, a group you are collaborating with can pick up on the project in Berlin. When they call it quits for the day, a third team can continue the effort in Chennai or Manila. While China and India continue to be major countries to which projects can be outsourced, outsourcing is also popular in countries like the Philippines and the Czech Republic. These foreign countries may have the type of talent you need to work on larger contracts.

A word to the wise would be to understand the business climate of these other countries. Make sure that you know how your copyright will be viewed overseas, and how to best protect it from being compromised. This may mean that you will need the services of an international lawyer to protect your intellectual property. It might also mean that you should hold onto the most important copyrighted material at the home office, while assigning less confidential elements to the foreign partners. However you decide to handle outsourcing, it may be quite useful to you. It is entirely possible that outsourcing will allow you to establish relationships abroad that may later be the source of profitable accounts. You shouldn't be quick to dismiss such possibilities.

You, Your Business, and the Law

When you were first starting down the entrepreneurial road, there were many legal issues that you weren't fully concerned about. You established yourself as a sole proprietor, and you may have been the only employee of your company. But the legal landscape changes as you grow. You will discover that certain protections and tax considerations will appear. As the size of your workforce grows, there are laws about equal employment opportunity that you must heed. Legislation is always a work in progress, and this means the laws will change periodically. Current laws that are due to expire may, at the last minute, be given extensions. Examining the laws of the states regarding small businesses would be a book in itself, so this eBook will concentrate on the national level and the statutes therein. Although you may be grinding your teeth and rolling your eyes about having to comply with various laws, do understand that not every one of them is meant to hold you back or delay your progress. Many are intended to help you.

A. Tax and Reporting Law

> It is natural to grumble about taxes, but please look on the bright side. The Obama Administration has enacted legislation that includes 18 different tax cuts that affect you and other small businesses. The Small Business Jobs Act, in particular, made eight tax cuts with small businesses in mind. The Affordable Care Act (a.k.a. Obamacare) will provide a small

business tax credit of up to 50% to a company with less than 25 full-time employees that provides health insurance. The Hiring Incentives to Restore Employment (Hire) Act will give you some tax incentives to hire previously unemployed individuals. The less-than-wonderful news is that an Internet Sales Tax is being discussed in the Marketplace Fairness Act. This would require a business that earns $1 million or more from Internet sales to collect taxes on all purchases (Faustman, 2013). It is still only being discussed, but do please keep this in mind.

You will be required to report to the Internal Revenue Service (IRS) with your income and expenses. You have, no doubt, been doing that, but your reporting requirements may change as you step up to a higher level in the business world. The accrual method of accounting, for example, may start to apply for you and your business. Reporting of finances is an effort by the government to maintain transparency, and your reporting may have to be in compliance with the Sarbanes Oxley Act (Lacoma, 2014)

This is where a POS system provides the maximum benefit for you. The data is collected in real time, and the reports are accurate. Tax compliance and financial reporting are made much easier, and your submissions will hold up better under any scrutiny. As you expand, you are going to discover that you will need the expertise of accounting professionals to keep up with the law and the reporting requirements. You should consider a local or regional accounting firm if you plan on using an outside accounting service. Think twice about using a one-person shop because of the risks involved. Should anything happen to that accountant, or if he or she closes down business, you could be stuck with a sizable hot mess. You may have to pick up the pieces, and you might be facing a tax audit all by yourself. A firm with a number of partners provides both stability and a records system that holds tax information from years gone by. If you are faced with an audit, the accounting firm can be called on to represent you, and that changes the dynamics considerably.

B. Employment and Equal Employment Opportunity

> The foundation stone of equal employment opportunity is fairness. There is a considerable amount of historical data to prove that, years ago, discrimination in employment was extensive, to the point of being quite casual. Equal employment opportunity (EEO) statutes are intended to prevent discrimination, and they also promote efficiency. By adhering to these laws, you are conditioning yourself to look for only the best-qualified candidates, and those attributes that are not work-related will not play a role in the hiring decision. It may come as a complete surprise to you, but you may be violating employment laws without even realizing what you are doing.
>
> These are rarely intentional and come as a result of not fully understanding the law. Exempt employees do not have to be

paid overtime, and some entrepreneurs will classify all employees as exempt. That can open up the possibility of being sued if an individual does not fully fit the criteria for being exempt. Litigation can also surface if you decide that all your employees are independent contractors. Non-compete agreements are not necessarily enforceable, and terminating an employee for taking military leave can lead to some serious trouble. The [US Department of Labor](#) provides information that can help a small business avoid making mistakes in the employment arena. It is definitely worth your while to review that employment knowledge.

> *SEE APPENDIX FOR NON-DISCRIMINATION POLICY EXAMPLE*

As you are reviewing the various laws governing employment and equal opportunity, here are several you should pay close attention to:

- The National Labor Relations Act
  This covers private employers engaged in interstate commerce. It is primarily concerned with collective bargaining and unions.

- The Americans with Disabilities Act
  This law prohibits discrimination against qualified individuals with disabilities.

- The Family and Medical Leave Act
  This law concerns itself with unpaid leave of absence for family- and/or health-related concerns.

- The Age Discrimination in Employment Act
  This protects individuals 40 years of age and older from employment discrimination based on age. This applies to employers with 20 or more employees.

- The Fair Credit Reporting Act
  This provides the guidelines for doing a background check on an employee or job applicant (Melanie Berkowitz, 2014).

C. The I-9

This form has to be completed to show that an employee has a lawful reason to be in the United States and can thus be hired. If you are in the restaurant or hospitality industries in particular, you must make sure that one of these forms is completed for each employee and is on file. A new version of the I-9 was issued by the Department of Homeland Security on March 8, 2013, and takes the place of any earlier forms.

A good idea is to do an audit of employee files to make sure the I-9 has been properly filled out. If a government audit shows noncompliance, fines as much as $900 or more can be levied for every violation (Bruce A. Coane, 2013).

D. Equal Employment Opportunity

Once you have a workforce of 15 employees working for 20 or more weeks a year for you, then Title VII of the Civil Rights Act of 1964 is something you need to pay close attention to. If, at the next step of your company's progress, you secure a federal contract, EEO compliance analyses will become a fact of business life.

It bears repeating that the cornerstone of equal employment opportunity is fairness. You are not allowed to discriminate in employment matters based on national origin, race, religion, color, sex, disability, or genetic information. Those employees who are over the age of 40 are to be treated the same way as those who are younger.

Perhaps one of the best ways to avoid any possibility of discrimination is to insist on zero tolerance for harassment. A good system of records-keeping for personnel will also be extremely important. There are various rules for the workplace that the equal employment opportunity commission oversees, and is a good idea to learn as much about them as possible. One such rule is to have EEO posters placed where employees can easily see them (e.g., the employee break room) (Agadoni, 2014). The Small Business Administration has a number of informational resources that will help you get better acquainted with the laws and regulations.

One thing that is very beneficial about equal employment opportunity is that it promotes high levels of efficiency. It has been proven time and again that discrimination is not an efficient way of doing business. Discrimination means that highly-qualified candidates are being overlooked because of any number of non-work-related issues, such as race or gender. The global economy of today is one of very firm competition. Every possible advantage has to be used. It is no coincidence that countries that practice high levels of discrimination are not the ones making advances. You can actually be a step or two ahead of your competition simply by practicing nondiscriminatory hiring and embracing the concept of a diverse workforce.

E. Changing the Business Registration

It is possible that you started your company as a sole proprietorship. That is understandable because it is very simple and direct. But, as you move to the next step, you may want to think about changing that business registration. A sole proprietorship puts your personal assets at risk, including bank accounts and the house you live in. Whether you go to a Limited Liability (LLC) or S Corporation or become fully incorporated is your personal decision, but these will all provide levels of security for your personal possessions.

- LLC
  The limited liability company, LLC, protects your personal assets. Debtors are able to go after the assets of the company, but must leave your private financial accounts alone. LLCs do not bear the burden of the double-taxation that hits both the company and any shareholder dividends. There is less paperwork with an LLC than with a corporation, and rules regarding shareholders aren't as stringent. Something to remember is that an LLC cannot go public. That will not be an initial problem if you are not planning an IPO. When the day comes that you do plan an IPO, however, you will have to re-register as a corporation (McCune, 2000).

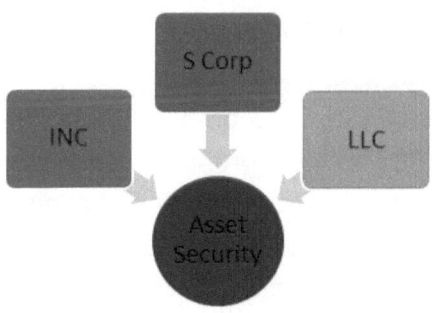

- S Corporation
  This is like the LLC in that your personal assets are not in danger. The S Corporation will offer a tax benefit when excess profits, or distributions, occur. If you have an S Corporation, you can pay your employees a "reasonable" salary and distribute profit in the form of dividends. These are taxed at a lower level than the income taxes. The guidelines are a bit stricter, and you need to be a United States citizen to qualify for this registration. While the S Corporation does allow for shareholders, there can be no more than one hundred, and there can be only one class of stock. The shareholders' interest in the company will determine how profits or losses are distributed in the S Corporation (Dahl, 2011).

- Incorporation
  An immediate benefit of incorporation is permanence for your company. A sole proprietorship ends at the death of the proprietor, and a partnership will dissolve when a partner leaves. Incorporation means that, regardless of what happens to the management, the company and its brand continue on. Just as with the other types of registration mentioned, your personal property is not put at risk.

  A marketplace advantage can be realized with incorporation. The permanence that is part of a corporation grants a legitimacy that cannot be found with the sole proprietorship. The brand is better protected because the law in most states prohibits other entities from using your trade name. Normal business expenses can be deducted before income is allocated to owners, and this includes salaries (NB. An LLC can also do this). An unlimited number of shareholders are allowed, and you need not be a United States citizen to have a corporation (Dealy, 2013).

Given these options, which one should you choose? The easy answer is that it is up to you. Here are some things you should ponder as you make your choice.

Sole proprietorship will probably not help you much at the next level. You need to be much more careful about the exposure of your assets as your business expands. It is possible that one type of registration will help you reward your subordinates better, but you may need to think of possibly raising money later with an IPO. Vendors are more inclined to do business with you at a different level of registration, and the company existence in spite of any management change may be important. There are also taxes and tax filing that have to be thought about. Sometimes, it can all be extremely confusing!

But guess what? These, in many ways, are the kinds of challenges you want to have. The business registration conundrum is evidence that your company is starting to take wing. What you should do is take a long look at your objectives for the coming years, particularly as they relate to the future need for additional fundraising. You may be able to work with just a few shareholders, or you might have to have a large number. Your management may or may not change based on your plans. The registration question is definitely an element of any business plan that peers into the future. At this point, you may want to seek help from outside consultants or attorneys on what to do. They will charge a fee, but their insights can help you make the right decision based on current needs and future objectives.

Conclusion

A lot of information has been shared with you in this eBook. Some of it may be new, and you may have already read about or heard about some of the other topics. However, you shouldn't treat any of this as idle chat. Everything is offered in the hopes that this knowledge will help you continue down the road to success.

Additionally, please think of this eBook as an encouragement to be receptive to change and innovation. The 21st century is a remarkable time for any small business owner. Software and social media applications are constantly being improved to better assist productivity and sales. You must stay informed about developments because you simply cannot be caught napping. The competition is always wide-awake.

Today's global economy can sometimes appear intimidating. However, it also presents opportunities for you and other small business owners that didn't exist at all at the turn of this new century. Technology and innovation do not rest. Newer and better productivity aids are even now in the process of being beta-tested and made ready for the marketplace. When William Shakespeare penned the words, "Oh, brave new world with such interesting people in it," he may well have been prophesying about you and your future business colleagues!

APPENDIX

TWITTER MARKETING TOOLS

Twitter is recognized as a great way to get the word out and to encourage people to check out your e-commerce site. Here are a few tools you can use to fine-tune your Twitter marketing effort:

- Tweriord (www.tweriord.com) This will analyze your both your tweets and your followers, allowing you to know the best time to post a tweet for marketing effect.

- Sproutsocial (www.sproutsocial.com) This will provide analytics and reports to give you a better picture of your Twitter followers.

- Trendsmap (www.trendsmap.com) This shows what topics are trending in a given region. You can find out more about the Twitter conversation in your area, as well as where you want to target marketing efforts.

- Twitalyzer (www.twitalyzer.com) This is considered a "one-stop shop" for all analytics requirements. It combines Twitter measures, demographic information, and Klout, among other metrics.

- Tweetreach (www.tweetreach.com) This gives a picture of how many people are sending out your marketing message;

- Bitly.com (www.bitly.com) This takes a URL and abbreviates it so that the address fits into Twitter's 140-character limit.

- Twittercounter (www.twittercounter.com) This measures the growth of your Twitter account and helps you chart the number of those following you and the statistics on those not following you.

- HootSuite (www.hootsuite.com) This allows you to schedule your tweets in advance, permitting you to optimize those hours of the day when your followers are online.

TOP CROWDFUNDING WEBSITES

Indiegogo.com (www.indiegogo.com)
RocketHub (www.rockethub.com)
PeerBackers (www.peerbackers.com)
Kickstarter (www.kickstarter.com)
SoMoLend (www.somolend)
Endurance Lending Network (www.enduranceln.com)
Grow Venture Community (www.growvc.com)
MicroVentures (www.microventures.com)
Angel List (https//angel.co)
CircleUp (https://circleup.com)

SOURCE: http://www.entrepreneur.com/article/228534

BIBLIOGRAPHY

Agadoni, L. (2014, September 30). *What is EEO Compliance?* Retrieved from www.smallbusiness.chron.com: http://smallbusiness.chron.com/eeo-compliance-44558.html

Arora, R. (2012, October 23). *7 Reasons to Avoid Crowdfunding.* Retrieved from www.smallbusiness.foxbusiness.com: http://smallbusiness.foxbusiness.com/finance-accounting/2012/10/23/7-reasons-to-avoid-crowdfunding/

Blackman, A. (2014, February 9). *Borrow or Lend Online-But Be Careful.* Retrieved from www.onine.wsj.com: http://online.wsj.com/news/articles/SB10001424052702303595404579318440300379408

Bruce A. Coane, E. (2013, August 23). *Form I-9: A Trap for Small Business.* Retrieved from www.sterlingeducation.com: http://www.sterlingeducation.com/the-sterling-blog/bid/95892/Form-I-9-A-Trap-for-Small-Business

Bullas, J. (2014, January 17). *22 Social Media Facts You Should Know in 2014.* Retrieved from www.jeffbullas.com: http://www.jeffbullas.com/2014/01/17/20-social-media-facts-and-statistics-you-should-know-in-2014/

Conner, C. (2014, March 4). *Ten Online Reputation Management Tips for Brand Marketers.* Retrieved from www.forbes.com:

http://www.forbes.com/sites/cherylsnappconner/2014/03/04/top-online-reputation-management-tips-for-brand-marketers/

Dahl, D. (2011, March 17). *Should Your Business Be an LLC or an S Corp?* Retrieved from www.inc.com: http://www.inc.com/guides/201103/s-corp-vs-llc.html

Dealy, E. (2013, January 31). *5 Reasons Why a Small Business Should Incorporate.* Retrieved from www.smallbusiness.foxbusiness.com: http://smallbusiness.foxbusiness.com/starting-a-business/2013/01/31/five-reasons-why-small-business-should-incorporate/

Fallon, N. (2014, July 2). *Crowdfunding Challenges Most Startups Don't Expect.* Retrieved from www.smallbusiness.foxbusiness.com: http://smallbusiness.foxbusiness.com/finance-accounting/2014/07/02/crowdfunding-challenges-most-startups-dont-expect/

Fallon, N. (2014, July 2). *Crowdfunding Challenges Most Startups Don't Expect.* Retrieved from www.smallbusiness.foxbusiness.com: http://smallbusiness.foxbusiness.com/finance-accounting/2014/07/02/crowdfunding-challenges-most-startups-dont-expect/

Faustman, M. (2013, August 6). *New Tax Laws Affecting Small Businesses and Startups.* Retrieved from blog.upcounsel.com: http://blog.upcounsel.com/new-tax-laws-affecting-small-businesses-and-startups/

Garling, C. (2014, September 23). *5 Best Mobile Apps for Managing Your Small to Medium Business.* Retrieved from www,webroot.com: http://www.webroot.com/us/en/business/resources/articles/mobile-security/5-best-mobile-apps-for-managing-your-small-to-medium-business

Gaul, B. (2013, December 11). *Gift Cards Increase Merchant Volume and Net Profits.* Retrieved from www.guardianlv.com: http://guardianlv.com/2013/12/gift-cards-increase-merchant-sales-volume-and-net-profits/

Goodman, M. (2012, June 11). *Case Study: How a Merchant Cash Advance Worked in a Pinch.* Retrieved from www.entrepreneur.com: http://www.entrepreneur.com/article/223523

Gray, I. A. (2014, September 26). *7 Reasons Why You SHOULD use Hootsuite.* Retrieved from www.iag.me: http://iag.me/socialmedia/reviews/7-reasons-why-you-should-use-hootsuite/

Lacoma, T. (2014, September 29). *Government Laws That Affect Businesses.* Retrieved from www.smallbusiness.chron.com: http://smallbusiness.chron.com/government-laws-affect-businesses-25756.html

LocalVox. (2014, January 22). *5 Fascinating Yelp Facts.* Retrieved from www.localvox.com: http://localvox.com/blog/5-fascinating-yelp-facts/

McCune, J. (2000, August 31). *Inc. Vs. LLC. Which Legal Structure Suits Your Business.* Retrieved from www.bankrate.com: http://www.bankrate.com/brm/news/biz/Biz_ops/20000831.asp

Melanie Berkowitz, E. (2014, September 30). *Small Business Guide: Five Important Laws to Know*. Retrieved from www.monster.com: http://hiring.monster.com/hr/hr-best-practices/workforce-management/employee-benefits-management/employment-laws.aspx

National Funding. (2013, September 4). *Lasting Effects: How the Great Recession Has Affected Small Businesses*. Retrieved from www.nationalfunding.com: https://www.nationalfunding.com/financing-lending/how-the-great-recession-has-affected-small-businesses/

New Zealand Herald. (2014, September 22). *These Four Apps Can Boost Productivity*. Retrieved from www.nzherald.co.nz: http://www.nzherald.co.nz/business/news/article.cfm?c_id=3&objectid=11329148

O'Hara, C. (2013, November 20). *10 Things You Need to Know About Online Reputation Management*. Retrieved from www.forbes.com: http://www.forbes.com/sites/learnvest/2013/11/20/10-things-you-need-to-know-about-online-reputation-management/

Rampton, J. (2014, March 29). *5 Reasons Your Business Should use AdWords*. Retrieved from www.forbes.com: http://www.forbes.com/sites/johnrampton/2014/03/29/5-reasons-your-business-should-use-adwords/

Retail Information Systems. (2014, September 26). *Benefits of Using A POS System*. Retrieved from www.armsys.com: http://www.armsys.com/art_benefits.html

Rose, J. (2013, April 26). *The Pros and Cons of a Merchant Cash Advance.* Retrieved from www.goodfinancialcents.com: http://www.goodfinancialcents.com/merchant-cash-advances/

Sareen, H. (2013, December 10). *Crowdfunding 2.0: A New Means for Capitalist Participation.* Retrieved from www,huffingtonpost.com: http://www.huffingtonpost.com/himanshu-sareen/crowdfunding-for-capitalist-participation_b_4379659.html

Smith, C. (2014, July 23). *LinkedIn May Not Be The Coolest Social Network, But It's Only Becoming More Valuable To Businesses.* Retrieved from www.businessinsider.com: http://www.businessinsider.com/demographic-data-and-social-media-2014-2

Tozzi, J. (2009, January 9). *How Merchant Cash Advances Work.* Retrieved from www.businessweek.com: http://www.businessweek.com/smallbiz/content/jan2009/sb2009018_234392.htm

Wuorio, J. (2014, September 26). *7 Reasons to Switch to a Point-of-Sale System.* Retrieved from www.microsoft.com: http://www.microsoft.com/business/en-us/resources/technology/business-software/7-reasons-to-switch-to-a-point-of-sale-system.aspx?fbid=zm0BNgl4pNS

www.ingramcontent.com/pod-product-compliance
Lightning Source LLC
Chambersburg PA
CBHW030734180526
45157CB00008BA/3161